FAMILY Life ISSUES

Maximizing Media

By Bruce Frederickson

CPH™
SAINT LOUIS

Editor: Rodney L. Rathmann
Editorial Assistant: Phoebe W. Wellman

This publication is also available in braille and in large print for the visually impaired. Write to Library for the Blind, 1333 S. Kirkwood Road, St. Louis, MO 63122-7295. Allow six months for processing.

Copyright © 1994 Concordia Publishing House
3558 S. Jefferson Avenue, St. Louis, MO 63118-3968
Manufactured in the United States of America

1 2 3 4 5 6 7 8 9 10   03 02 01 00 99 98 97 96 95 94

Contents

Introduction   5

1 Media, Messages, and My Family   9

2 The Great Escape   17

3 Think about Such Things!   25

4 What about Censorship?   33

5 It is Written   41

6 Evaluating Media   49

Leader Notes   57

   Session 1   57

   Session 2   61

   Session 3   65

   Session 4   68

   Session 5   72

   Session 6   76

Introduction

▲ About *Maximizing Media*

This course has been especially prepared for use in a small group setting by adults who are concerned about honoring God in their use of media. It may, however, also be used as a self study or taught in a traditional Sunday morning Bible class.

▲ Planning for a Small Group Study

1. *Select a leader* for the course or a leader for the day. It will be the leader's responsibility to secure needed materials, to keep the discussion moving, and to help involve everyone.

2. *Emphasize sharing.* Your class will work best if the participants feel comfortable with one another and if all feel that their contributions to the class discussion are important and useful. Take the necessary time at the beginning of the course to get to know one another. You might share names, occupations, hobbies, etc. Share what you expect to gain from this course.

Invite participants to bring photos of their families to the first session to pass around as they introduce themselves and tell about the individual members of their families. Be open and accepting. Don't force anyone to speak. The course will be most helpful if participants willingly share deep feelings, problems, doubts, fears, and joys. That will require building an atmosphere of openness, trust, and caring about one another. Take time to build relationships among participants. That time will not be wasted!

3. Help participants apply the concepts included in each session. After each week's study, there is a suggested activity.

An old Chinese proverb summarizes the "why?" of the activity:

> I hear and I forget;
>
> I see and I remember;
>
> I do and I understand.

The activity is to help families do and thus understand. Encourage everyone to take time to do it.

4. Encourage participants to invite their friends—including their unchurched friends—to be a part of this study.

▲ As You Plan to Lead the Group

1. Read this guide in its entirety before you lead the first session.

2. Use the Leader Notes found in the back of this guide.

3. Pray each day for those who join the group.

4. As you prepare for each session, study the Bible texts thoroughly. Work through the exercises for yourself. Depend on the Holy Spirit. Expect His presence; He will guide you and cause you to grow. God will not let His Word return empty (Isaiah 55:11) as you study it both individually and with the others in the group.

5. Do not expect the Spirit to do your work for you. Start early. Prepare well. As time permits, do additional reading about the topic.

6. Begin and end with prayer.

7. Begin and end on time. Punctuality is a courtesy to everyone and can be a factor that will encourage discussion and attendance.

8. Find ways to keep the session informal. Meet in casual surroundings. Arrange seating so participants can face one another. Ask volunteers to provide refreshments.

9. Keep the class moving. Move the class along from section to section in the Study Guide. Limit your discussion to questions of interest to the participants. Be selective. You don't need to cover every question and every Bible verse.

10. Try to build one another up through your fellowship and study. You have your needs; other group members have theirs. Together you have a lot to gain.

11. Be sensitive to any participants who may have needs related to the specific problems discussed in this course, especially anyone who may need Christian counseling and professional help.

12. Be a "gatekeeper." That means you may need to shut the gate on one person while you open it for someone else. Try to involve everyone, especially those who hesitate to speak.

▲ If You Are Using This Study on Your Own

1. Each time you sit down to study a session, ask the Holy Spirit for guidance and counsel. Expect Him to work through His Word to encourage, motivate, and empower you to grow a little more like Jesus.

2. Study the Bible texts, printed in the course, with special care. God works through His Word. In it you will find power. Read each text slowly, several times.

3. Write answers in the spaces provided. Avoid the temptation just to "think" your responses. Writing will force you to be specific. It's in that specificity you are most likely to identify crucial issues for yourself. Check the leaders notes in the back of this guide for information you may find helpful as you go along.

4. Pray as you work. Ask God to show you what He wants you to see about Him, about yourself, and about your family situation.

Media, Messages, and My Family

1

Opening Devotion

Begin by reading Psalm 119:105. God's Word is both a lamp to show the way and a light to draw attention to obstacles in our path. From others in your group, draw insights about how God's Word is important as a lamp and a light. Pray thanking God for His gift of His word. Ask for the blessing of His Holy Spirit upon your study.

What Is Media?

The dictionary defines media (the plural of medium) as a means of communication.

1. Other than to communicate, what purpose do media serve?

2. List as many forms of media as you can think of in one minute.

3. List several ways in which media affects your family (positive and negative).

The Changing Family

Just as there are different types of media, there are also many different types of family. How many different family configurations can you name?

According to Dr. Carl J. Moser of the Board for Parish Services of the LCMS, the percentage of U. S. households which are made up of married couples with children under 18 has decreased from over 40% in 1970 to 25% in 1993. In the same time period, people living alone has increased by eight percent and the number of single mothers with children has nearly doubled. Approximately 28% of all births are by unmarried women, up from five percent in 1960.

As God's Great Commission-minded people, concerned about bringing the saving gospel of Jesus Christ to all people, we must rely upon the guidance and direction of the Holy Spirit as we plan to bring God's Word—Law and Gospel—to families of all forms, including many that are not like ours.

1. How has media influenced society's ideas about families and family life?

2. Relate the positive and negative aspects of society's acceptance of the changing shapes of families.

3. How have changes in families affected the church?

4. God has planned for men and women to join together in marriage as a lifelong union for purposes of mutual support and enjoyment and for the procre-

ation and nurture of children. As the Holy Spirit empowers us, how can God's people effectively minister to persons forming households that are inconsistent with God's plan for family life?

Media and Our Way of Life

Media inspires, entertains, and communicates, providing us with pertinent information about ourselves and the world around us.

The amount of information available to us is literally exploding. The amount of knowledge is doubling every 20 years, and the span of time it takes for media to double is decreasing every year.

1. List several examples of media that are readily available to members of your family, within your home, and in places outside your home.

2. Many of us use very little of the vast amount of media available to us. Comment on the various types of media available and their value to you and your family.

3. Who makes decisions about kinds of media available to members of your family? Are some decisions made by default rather than through an informed and deliberate process?

4. Do you and others in your family ever feel like you are being bombarded by media? Explain.

▼

5. What guideline(s) do you and your family have or could you adopt to help you make informed and deliberate decisions about media selection and usage.

▲▲▲▲▲▲▲▲▲▲▲▲▲▲▲▲▲▲▲▲▲▲▲▲▲▲▲

"No TV Night"

In order to encourage use of alternate media, establish a "no TV night" during which the family finds something else to do. Everyone might do his or her own thing or family members might do something together such as playing a game or taking turns reading for 15 minutes to other family members.

▼▼▼▼▼▼▼▼▼▼▼▼▼▼▼▼▼▼▼▼▼▼▼▼▼▼

Media and You

Imagine that your house is burning. Everyone is safe outside your home, but all of your possessions remain inside. What items would you rescue?

1. List five of these items.

2. Would any of the objects you would consider saving be media?

3. What do they communicate to you, and why are they so important to you?

4. God's Word is the most important message to ever be communicated through the use of media. 2 Kings 22 records the account of a time when God's Word was neglected. King Josiah had ordered a repair of the temple. During the restoration project,

the workmen discovered a lost book of the Law. Distressed that such an important thing as God's Law had been misplaced, the King, Josiah, immediately ordered that the book be read to all the people. To his horror he discovered that he and his people had *not* been living according to God's Word and will.

Give examples of how people neglect God's Word today. Refer to the First (You shall have no other gods.), Second (You shall not take the name of the Lord your God in vain.), and Third (Remember the Sabbath Day to keep it holy.) Commandments.

5. Explain how Ephesians 1:7 applies to all who feel sorrow over their neglect of the most important message ever communicated.

6. According to the following, for what purpose do people continue to communicate God's Word?
   a. John 20:31

   b. 2 Timothy 3:16

7. Through Christ's life, death, and resurrection, God has touched our lives forever. He sent us an eternal message that He loves and cares for us. In Christ we are acceptable to God. Which media *best* communicate the Good News of Christ?

8. What are some of the things or forces that stand in the way of God's Word and the message of Good News in Christ?

13
▼

9. What are some of the things that you could do so that the Good News—Christ's victory for us over sin and death—could *best* be communicated?

Share a Word

What is your favorite Bible verse? Is it marked in your Bible? Do you have it committed to memory? How is it useful to you? When do you use it? Have you ever shared it with someone else?

1. My favorite Bible verse is

2. This verse is special to me because

3. To me these words mean that

4. Paul reminded Timothy of his mother and grandmother who had taught him about Jesus as a child. What are some of the earliest memories you have of being taught about Jesus? When do these memories come back to you?

5. If you have children, how can you help to create some of these same memories for them? If you are involved in teaching children, or adults, how could you help encourage them to read the Bible regularly?

6. If you don't read the Bible at a regular time each day/week, why not begin today? Have you ever thought about reading through the entire Bible? Why

not consider the following and invite someone else to join you.

First choose a version of the Bible that you will continue to use each day for this project. Consider using a modern translation which may make your reading easier. It is especially helpful if you choose a Bible with wider margins so you can take notes as you go along. You might also want to keep a notebook close by to take notes of interesting things you encountered during your reading. Now, by reading only three chapters a day and five on Sunday, you can read through the entire Bible in just one year. Here's how you do it.

▲▲▲▲▲▲▲▲▲▲▲▲▲▲▲▲▲▲▲▲▲▲▲▲▲▲

On Monday, read the first three chapters of Genesis and continue reading three chapters a day each Monday until you complete Genesis. Then go into Exodus and continue reading on Mondays until you have completed Deuteronomy.

On Tuesday, begin reading the first three chapters of Joshua and continue reading three chapters in Joshua each Tuesday until you have completed it. Then go on to Judges and continue reading on Tuesdays all the way through Esther.

On Wednesdays, read three chapters in Job and continue through Proverbs.

On Thursdays, read three chapters in Isaiah and continue through Malachi.

On Fridays, read three chapters in Matthew and continue reading through John.

On Saturdays, read three chapters in Acts and continue through Revelation.

On Sundays, read *five* chapters anywhere in the Bible. Perhaps there is one section in which you were particularly interested in during the past week. Or perhaps there is a place where you got behind and would like to get caught up.

▼▼▼▼▼▼▼▼▼▼▼▼▼▼▼▼▼▼▼▼▼▼▼▼▼

When you finish each day's reading, make a pencil notation of the date in the margin of your Bible so you will know where to pick up again next week. Erase the mark when you begin and remark the margin when you complete your reading.

May God bless you as you stay close to Him through the reading of His Word! And of course as you are listening to God speak to you, it will seem quite natural to speak to Him in prayer. Share the secrets of your heart—your burdens and your joys. Your relationship with God will grow stronger. And your appreciation of one of the most important media will grow.

Closing Meditation

Read the Great Commission, Matt. 28:18–20. Rejoice together that God has invited us to share His Good News. In prayer, thank God for media, especially the message of the Gospel, and for families in which to share the wonderful promises that He gives. Ask for the power of His Spirit to enable us to bring the message of God and His love to others.

During the Week

Read *The Wretched Stone* by Chris Van Allsburg, (Houghton Mifflin Co., Boston, 1991). This book is readily available in a public or school library. It describes what happens to the crew of a ship when they discover this large "stone" on a deserted island. One side of the stone, which is about 2 feet square, is as smooth as glass and a strange and intriguing light emanates from it. Gradually all the crew members abandon their posts to stare at this strange stone, until they are in danger of shipwreck. After reading the story (together with some excellent pictures), discuss what the stone represents. How did the ship's crew react to the stone? Is their reaction realistic? How and when did "recovery" from the strange effects of the stone take place? This book would also be an excellent story to read to children.

The Great Escape

2

Opening Meditation

Read 1 Corinthians 12:4–6, 12. Each person has unique gifts, yet together we all make up a unit called the body of Christ. Not everyone can sing and dance, and we can't all be athletes. The source of our gifts is the grace of our Lord Jesus Christ. We might be tempted to think we have these gifts simply to satisfy our own desires, but according to v. 7, God has gifted us for the good of *everyone*! Invite reactions and involve your group in spontaneous prayer, thanking God for the many and varied gifts He has given in order to build up the body of Christ.

Media

Place a + before each of the following statements with which you agree. Place a — before each of the following with which you disagree.

_____1. Television keeps me company.

_____2. Going to movies is a great form of entertainment, especially with good acting and an action-packed plot.

_____3. I couldn't function with out my computer and modem.

_____4. The newspaper keeps me informed. In our family we read and discuss the paper together.

_____5. On the average, people who watch television live longer than those who don't.

_____6. Playing the radio in the car is okay when I'm by myself, but it inhibits meaningful communication between me and my children when we are riding in the car together.

_____7. I get annoyed when I am visiting someone and they refuse to turn off the television in the background.

_____8. Turning up the stereo in my room helps me to feel in control of my environment.

_____9. There's nothing I enjoy more than curling up at night with a magazine or a good book.

_____10. Television programs give my family something to talk about. We discuss what we watch on TV.

Two Perspectives

Media has done much to enhance the human experience. It brings us firsthand information from around the world, enabling us to witness history unfolding. It makes us laugh and cry. It causes us to wonder at life in other times and places. It helps us to feel with and for others as they face the challenges, uncertainties, and struggles of life. Media reinforces, molds, and shapes attitudes and values as it models standards of behavior.

Jesus lived, died, and rose again to provide us with the forgiveness of sins and a new and eternal life in Him. When we come to faith, His Spirit makes us new. Working through the Word He changes us, bringing our thoughts, words, and actions into conformity with those that are pleasing to God.

Together with a partner apply each of the following to influences media has and can have in families, who by the Spirit's power, desire to live their lives in praise, thanks, and obedience to God. Look for positive as well as negative applications.

1. Be imitators of God, therefore, as dearly loved children and live a life of love, just as Christ loved us and gave Himself up for us as a fragrant offering and sacrifice to God. But among you there must not be even a hint of sexual immorality, or any kind of impurity, or of greed, because these are improper for God's holy people. Nor should there be obscenity, foolish talk or coarse joking, which are out of place, but rather thanksgiving (Ephesians 5:1–4).

2. So whether you eat or drink or whatever you do, do it all for the glory of God (1 Corinthians 10:31).

3. Since, then, you have been raised with Christ, set your hearts on things above, where Christ is seated at the right hand of God. Set your minds on things above, not on earthly things. For you died, and your life is now hidden with Christ in God (Colossians 3:1–3).

4. Do not love the world or anything in the world. If anyone loves the world, the love of the Father is not in him. For everything in the world—the cravings of sinful man, the lust of his eyes and the boasting of what he has and does—comes not from the Father but from the world. The world and its desires pass

away, but the man who does the will of God lives forever   (1 John 2:15–17).

5. Finally, . . . whatever is true, whatever is
noble, whatever is right, whatever is pure, whatever
is lovely, whatever is admirable—if anything is excellent or praiseworthy—think about such things
(Philippians 4:8).

Wise Use of Media

As with any powerful force, media and the influence we allow them to have in our lives and our families must be controlled. Media teaches and models
standards of behavior that come to be regarded as
acceptable by many, especially by the young and vul-
nerable. Recently the newspapers carried a story
about a five-year-old child who started the fire that
killed his infant sister. The five-year-old claimed that
he had learned from a controversial cable television
show, designed for teenagers, that "fire is cool!"

Since 1976, the American Medical Association
has been concerned about offering a warning about
television violence, insisting that "television violence
is an environmental hazard threatening the health
and welfare of young Americans and indeed our
future society."

While serving and since retiring as Surgeon General of the United States, C. Everett Koop has been
an outspoken critic of television violence, as were the
generals before him. "I think it is time for the net-
works and for individual stations to be candid with
themselves and with the American people. They

dwell far too much on the dark side of human nature for a number of unpardonable reasons; it is sensational . . . it is easy to do . . . it can be done quickly and cheaply by writers and producers of little talent . . . and it requires no sympathetic knowledge of the human spirit!" (*Christianity Today*)

For years the National Parent-Teacher Association has encouraged schools to teach children to become skilled, critical consumers of media, rather than passive recipients of whatever television and other media forms have to offer. Grace Baisinger of the National PTA has said "We are not teaching analysis of the media the way we do literature and art." (*Christianity Today*)

According to Dr. Henry Gault, M.D., child psychiatrist at one of our nations leading hospitals, the typical teenager, by age 18, has spent more time (between 15,000 and 20,000 hours) watching television, than he or she has spent in school (only about 11,000 hours).

The *Kid Vid Guide* produced by the Littleton, Colorado, Parent's Teacher's Organization makes specific suggestions for alternatives to excessive TV watching and overinvolvement in other forms of media: Television can be the quick answer to entertainment, a cheap babysitter, and something to "keep the kids occupied" while parents are involved in adult activities. They suggest some alternatives and invite you to add your own.

A partial list of activities which provide worthy alternatives to television includes: reading books; playing games; taking walks; riding bikes; being outdoors; going to museums, libraries, the zoo, or the planetarium; writing a story; writing in a diary; writing letters to pen pals, grandparents, or to or for a newspaper. You may help around the house, help an elderly neighbor or relative or younger child. You may do puzzles; draw pictures; build models; make scrap arts; swim, skate; join a team, a club; or simply sit still, or talk with a parent or sibling. The possibilities are endless, while TV and video games are very limiting.

1. Do you agree with the American Medical Asso-

ciation that "television violence is an environmental hazard threatening the health and welfare of young Americans and indeed our future society"? Why or why not?

2. How could we, as Christians concerned about the influence of media in our families, and in society as a whole, help promote a wholesome use of media?

3. What can we do to equip our families, and especially our children, to analyze, evaluate, and select from among the variety of media's offerings?

During the Week

1. If you decide you want to make changes in your child's use of any media, join them in its use for one week. Pay attention to how they choose a particular program or game. Ask them *why* they made certain choices. Sit down together and discuss limits—remembering that children very often mimic the habits of significant adults. Keep a time log of each media usage. Most people will be surprised at the great amount of time they spend with media, compared to interpersonal communication! Agree to join other family members in monitoring their use of media. Discuss your findings in future study meetings and plan strategies together.

2. Have each family member list their three favorite television or radio programs. Create a master list on a piece of paper. Talk about what makes a

person successful: money, possessions, friends, prestigious position, wholesome values, a friendly and helpful family, etc. Try to come to agreement about what makes an individual successful. Then prioritize the programming, and create a new list in which the programming that best characterizes success appears on the top. Discuss the characterization of Christians, the church, or clergy in any of the programming. Discuss alternatives which would better support your values.

3. As an alternative to television and other media that provide input from the outside, agree to set aside an hour each week in which the family comes together simply to enjoy one another's company. Possible activities to pursue during your time together include the following: recreate a radio broadcast such as the kind your grandparents listened to when they were little, take turns reading a story aloud to each other, or create a family variety show, providing a "microphone," and several chairs for an audience (which may even be any family member who is not presently speaking). Tape or better yet, videotape your production for lots of laughs later.

4. Read Ephesians 3:14–19 for your family devotions one night this week. Emphasize the family words. Talk about ways in which the church is like a family. Talk about the strengths of your church. Then compare these to strengths found in families. Talk about ways in which relationships can grow and improve.

5. Join other families for a designated period of time during which you turn off the television or deliberately avoid another particular type of media. Provide ways in which participating families can support each other. Provide lists of specific alternatives that could occupy the time otherwise spent with media. At the end of a "TV Tune Out," have families respond to the following:

a. List some activities your family did during the tune out.

b. Are any of these new activities ones that you would like to become a part of your family's regular routine?

c. What important thing did you learn from the "tune-out"?

d. If you could change this activity in the future, what recommendations would you make?

6. Talk about how movies have changed over the last 20 years, and what *you* can do about it. Do you think pickets or boycotts operated by such groups as the National Federation for Decency are successful in effecting positive change? Why or why not?

Closing Meditation

Read a portion of Paul's farewell speech to the elders of the church in Ephesus in Acts 20:28. Paul spoke these words as he was leaving, aware that he might never see these close friends again. He reminds them of the responsibility that God the Holy Spirit has placed upon them. They are to keep watch over those in their care. While everyone may not have direct responsibility for children and others, all of us are citizens of a city, county, state, and nation, in which decisions are made. Close with prayer, asking for God's wisdom and guidance in demonstrating care and concern for the souls of others.

Think about Such Things! ▼ **3**

Opening Meditation

Read what the aged Simeon *said* when he first *saw* the Christ child, Luke 2:25–35. He was delighted to *see* this visible sign of the presence of God's saving grace. Simeon *saw* the Christ Child and rejoiced. What *sight* causes you to rejoice? In prayer thank God for all forms of media, and ask for wisdom in knowing how to deal with the unpleasantness and violence contained in some media.

A Threat to Society

National Football Hall of Famer Walter Payton recently said, "You know who is raising our kids? TV. It's the worst thing in the world for kids. When you have kids, please take all of your TVs out of your house or at least lock them up."

1. What is your *initial* reaction to Payton's statement?

2. *Why* do you think Payton made such a *strong* statement?

3. *Why* do you agree or disagree with Payton?

4. Would you ever go so far as to "lock up" your televisions? Explain.

5. How would you react to someone who did?

Sex and Violence in Media

Ever since the fall of Adam and Eve into sin, we have lived in a world of violence. The Bible speaks of murder, wars, and many acts of violence. Because of our sin-contaminated condition, we find actions that bring hurt, damage, and suffering into the lives of others.

The enjoyment of violence has followed humanity throughout its history. In the early days of Roman empire thousands of people assembled to witness the torture and death of Christians who were herded into arenas before the release of hungry lions. During the Civil War the genteel of Washington took carriage rides complete with picnic meals to watch the battles taking place a short distance from the capital city.

In our contemporary world both electronic and printed media include a great deal of violent words and images. On the nightly TV news live coverage of wars and strife in third-world nations together with vivid images of death and disaster from our own cities constantly bombard our senses.

According to a recent issue of *USA Today*, in television comedy programming, there is a joke about sex every four minutes. Eighty-five percent of all jokes in comedies on television relate to sex. Sex on television is usually between unmarried couples. Of 45 sex scenes in a typical week, only four are between married heterosexuals.

1. Should the images of war and murder and sex-

uality that are allowed into our media be regulated? Why or why not? Who should assume the responsibility for this regulation?

2. Research indicates that persons exposed to violence and sexually explicit material become desensitized after a period of time to what might initially shock or abhor them. How can we, as consumers of media, avoid the desensitization to actions that dishonor God according to the standards He has established for us (Ten Commandments)?

3. In addition to ignoring violence, or speaking out boldly against it, what alternatives do you believe a Christian has today?

4. Talk about what steps *you* have already taken to *limit* or control the way violence or sexually explicit matter enters your sphere of influence.
   a. What *forces* would work against limiting violence in your home?

b. What kind of guidance should children receive about the literature they purchase or check out from the library? How do you determine what material is appropriate for children in your home or school? Do you trust age-level suggestions that the media itself makes, or do you typically exercise some kind of guidance?

c. Distinguish between the violent sources over which you have control, and those over which you have absolutely no control. What can you do?

How Do You Picture Jesus?

Most people think of Jesus as a kindly, gentle person. Once He invited children to sit on His lap, even against the wishes of His closest friends and disciples (Mark 10:13–16).

1. How do you picture Jesus? What scenes would you film if you were making a movie about Jesus?

2. Consider whether the scenes you chose, or your memories about Jesus, are mostly gentle or violent, and explain why you think you chose one over the other.

3. God is love (1 John 4:8). How do you reconcile God who is the essence of love and who desires the salvation of everyone (1 Timothy 2:4) with several of His acts of destruction mentioned in the Bible (e.g., destroying the world He had made in a flood [Genesis 6–9] or sending His angel to put to death 185,000 men in the Assyrian army [Isaiah 37:36])?

4. Are there two sides of God's love? If so, how do God's *hard* and *soft* sides differ?

5. Consider two very graphic Bible stories—the mauling of 42 youths from Bethel after Elisha called down the curse of the Lord upon them for showing disdain for him as the Lord's representative (2 Kings 2:23–24) and the narrative recorded in Judges 19 of a women who dies after being raped by the men of the city. Some atheists have protested the reading of the Bible in public schools because they say it is a violent, sexually explicit book. How would you explain this criticism of God's holy Word?

God's Gifts

The fall of humanity into sin brought catastrophic results. Because of the sin of our first parents, people find themselves at odds with God and with each other. Nature also experienced the results of the fall. Animals began to prey upon each other and to contend with humanity; and both plants and animals found themselves in conflict with people.

But God did not leave His creation in this desperate state. He sent a Savior—His only Son—who came to earth to bring peace, restoring the relationship between God and humanity through His life, death, and resurrection.

1. God's Word describes the type of peace Jesus brings to lives held under the curse of sin who turn to Him. Listed below are two passages that talk about this peace that only Jesus can provide. Share with a partner what each of these passages means to you.

a. The wolf will live with the lamb, the leopard will lie down with the goat, the calf and the lion and the yearling together; and a little child will lead them. The cow will feed with the bear, their young will lie down together, and the lion will eat straw like the ox. The infant will play near the hole of the cobra, and the young child put his hand into the viper's nest. They will neither harm nor destroy on all my holy mountain, for the earth will be full of the knowledge of the LORD as the waters cover the sea (Isaiah 11:6–9).

b. And the peace of God, which transcends all understanding, will guard your hearts and your minds in Christ Jesus (Philippians 4:7).

2. All who know Jesus as their Lord and Savior can know the kind of peace described in the passages

above—even while living in the midst of violence, hostility, and turmoil. Knowing such peace, Christian martyrs went to their death confident in their Savior's love and care. Until Jesus comes to bring the world to an end, God's people must contend with the continuing violence in a world contaminated by sin. Until that time comes, God's people possess an additional gift from God.

Read Romans 8:18–25 to a partner. Identify and comment on the presence of that gift in the life of a follower of Christ.

God's Presence in the Lives of His People

In Colossians 3, Paul writes about the difference God desires to make in the lives of those who by faith belong to Him. Read and discuss verses 1–17 with a partner or in a group of three or four.

1. How do verses 1–4 describe the difference that can occur in lives of those who possess saving faith in Jesus?

2. Make a short list of the evidence of the old self and the new self in the lives of people who trust in Jesus for salvation.
Old Self (vv. 3:5–9)

New Self (vv. 10–17)

3. As the Holy Spirit works in the lives of His people through their study of the Word and in their participation in the Sacraments, God brings us to desire to honor Him in the lives we live and in the things we allow to influence us.

If you have decided that you want in your life the peace to which God has called you (v. 15), think for a moment about your use of media.

a. What are some media experiences and decisions that would encourage and support God's peace in your life?

b. What media experiences discourage this kind of peace and tranquility in your life?

c. When encountering any media, print or nonprint, informational or entertainment, what personal rule could you draw from verse 17?

4. Athletes find it helpful to see themselves as winners before competing and then to follow through in a postive and confident manner as they enter the competition itself. Reflecting on these verses from Colossians 3, how would God have you apply these techniques from athletic competition to your Christian life?

▼

During the Week

1. Suggest that families watch a TV cartoon together. Every time someone gets hurt, say ouch! Tally those ouches. Are some cartoons less violent than others?

2. Take the television listings from the newspapers and invite family members to circle those programs which tend to be more violent. Discuss the results of the violent acts often seen on television. Discuss the negative results of seeing violence on TV, including the news. How often is violence used as a method of problem solving? Do real people solve problems in this way? What are the alternatives?

3. Compile a list of the names and addresses of the program directors for local television and the radio stations your young people watch or listen to the most.

4. With your group create a report card for media sources to which your family is exposed. On the report card provide room, for example, for the name of the program and its sources, why you chose to watch the program, good points, bad points, and give it a grade, A, B, C, D, or F, just like in school. It would be interesting if each family member did this individually, and then compared their results. If you are studying in a group, consider bringing your results back to the group next time.

Closing Meditation

Read Genesis 1:1–13, and contrast the power necessary to create the world and all that is in it, with the gentleness necessary to create the delicate plants and animals. Now read vv. 26–31, and close with a prayer of thanks that God created people to praise Him and enjoy His creation.

What about Censorship? 4 ▼

Opening Meditation

Think about the senses God has given you—the abilities to see, hear, touch, taste, and smell. Why do you think God gave these beautiful gifts to you? Consider how someone without one of these senses is limited. We show that we value these senses by protecting them. For example, we protect our eyes from bright lights and our ears from extremely loud sounds. Similarly, God would have us protect ourselves for other influences that would harm us. Begin this session with a prayer asking God for wisdom to approach all we "see" and "do" so that we may do all things to His glory (1 Corinthians 10:31).

Think on Those Things!

Long ago, a clever military general, figured out a way to defeat his enemies who were barricaded inside their walled city. He hid a few soldiers inside a large wooden horse. This horse was built on wheels and set before the city gates late one night. In the morning the curious people inside saw the horse and quickly wheeled it into their city fortress. All day long they admired this new gift and congratulated themselves on bringing it inside the city.

When night fell and everyone was asleep, the hidden soldiers sneaked out from their hiding place inside the horse, opened the city gates from the inside, and allowed the rest of the army in. They easily defeated the sleeping enemies.

This well-known story of the Trojan horse,

demonstrates an important truth. When we are tempted and sin, we have no one to blame but ourselves, though we may be inclined to blame someone else—even God—for our wrongdoing. But like the enemy that sprung out from the Trojan horse, sin begins inside us as Matthew's gospel records, "For out of the heart come evil thoughts, murder, adultery, sexual immorality, theft, false testimony, slander" (Matthew 15:19).

So how do we shake off evil? Only by the power of Jesus can we break free of the evil that springs up within us. By His death and resurrection, Jesus defeated the devil. Through His Word, which He left among us, Jesus gives us the Spirit's power to resist the temptations of the devil, the world, and our own sinful flesh. Through the power of the Gospel we are able to avoid the luring appeal of evil and to focus instead on "whatever is true, whatever is noble, whatever is right, whatever is pure, whatever is lovely, whatever is admirable . . . excellent or praiseworthy" (Philippians 4:8).

Controlling What Is Seen and Heard

Do you believe in censorship? Consider each of the following examples.

• (234–149 B. C.) Cato the Elder, consul and censor, determined what reached the senses of the average Roman citizen. Leaders hoped to "protect" their citizens from potentially dangerous foreign customs and ideas.

• (1511–53) Michael Servetus did not believe in the doctrines of the Trinity and infant Baptism, and was ultimately burned at the stake by those who wanted to stop the spread of his ideas.

• In 1842 as part of the Tariff Acts, it became illegal to bring "indecent and obscene" materials into the United States. For all their sincerity, these lawmakers ignored materials which were produced locally. They also failed to point out who would determine local standards of decency.

• By 1957, the U.S. Supreme Court had decided that the First Amendment freedom of expression did not extend to obscenity. By 1973, the Supreme Court was called upon to assist in determining just what was obscenity. The high court indicated that while local governments could certainly differ in their definitions of prohibited materials, their guidelines must define the socially redeeming value of materials considered obscene in one place and not in another.

• In 1992 a superintendent of a public school district in a midwestern state forbid the use of the word Christmas in the December school program. Whenever a song was sung containing the offending word, students sang the word *censored* instead. The rule was later repealed.

1. Cato the Elder served as censor in order to protect Roman citizens from potentially dangerous foreign customs and ideas. How do you feel about investing so much power in one person? Do you think censorship is effective in stopping the spread of ideas, such as those religious or political in nature?

2. Do you think media should be censored? If so, how widely should guidelines extend?

3. If censorship occurs, *who* do you believe should be the censors?

4. How do you feel about the statement "censorship begins at home"?

▼

5. Consider each of the following Bible references. What direction for limiting what others may be allowed to look at or experience through public media is included in each?

Test everything. Hold on to the good. Avoid every kind of evil (1 Thessalonians 5:21–22).

Love must be sincere. Hate what is evil; cling to what is good (Romans 12:9).

Have you been thinking all along that we have been defending ourselves to you? We have been speaking in the sight of God as those in Christ; and everything we do, dear friends, is for your strengthening (2 Corinthians 12:19).

Let us therefore make every effort to do what leads to peace and to mutual edification (Romans 14:19).

Responsibility and the Right of Choice

Some parents may prevent young children from seeing movies that depict violence or explicit sex, only to discover that they are exposed to the same kinds of things in the television news. These parents may find themselves questioning whether they are old fashioned or unjustly shielding their children from reality.

Though books, movies, and television programs, depicting premarital and extramarital sexual relations may be realistic among certain segments of society, concerned Christian parents find themselves asking, is it helpful for my children to be exposed to this reality at this time in their lives?

Censorship laws have been written for two reasons: to protect "from" and protect "to."

Censorship laws that protect certain individuals "from" being exposed to certain media, also protect them "to" be able to enjoy others.

The issues surrounding the subject of censorship cannot be dealt with in a simplistic fashion. It would be too easy to say, "Just prohibit all pictures of naked bodies and all materials which contain obscene language." Consider certain art forms.

Some forms of media might be considered objectionable not because of their content, but according to the purpose for which the communication takes place. For example, the display of a nude body in one place may be objectionable, but in another quite acceptable. Paintings and sculptures in museums may feature images that in another context might exploit both the subject and the consumer. Intent is important.

Some materials, while the product of the freedom of expression by one individual, may not be uplifting or helpful to another. What would prevent someone else from prohibiting those things which *you* enjoy and value? If you could eliminate from print certain words that you consider objectionable, *what* and *who* would prevent someone else from eliminating the name of Jesus or the Word of God, now or in the future? Remember, it has been tried!

Everyone practices some kind of censorship, based either on what they feel is *acceptable*, or what they *like*. Those in authority, who exercise censorship over others, must do so carefully and reverently aware of their awesome responsibility. "Obey your leaders and submit to their authority. They keep watch over you as men who must give an account" (Hebrews 13:17). Authority can easily be abused, especially when the person in authority is not motivated by the love of God.

1. Why and how can Christian parents and others in positions of authority legitimately limit the media sources that others receive?

2. Recall that in the history of censorship, laws were created to prohibit obscene materials from being brought into our country. Similar laws exist about what can be sold. But what about the possession of materials which are homemade? Do you believe that censorship laws and guidelines should extend to ownership as well as the import and sale of objectionable materials?

3. What is the difference between the pictures of naked people depicted on the pages of *Playboy* or *Playgirl* magazine, as compared to similar pictures in *National Geographic*? If you were writing censorship guidelines, would you make a distinction, and if so, how?

4. How important do you believe it is to limit certain media to a particular age group? Consider the rating of films, or the recommendations of certain magazines "for adults only." Do you believe these are effective guidelines or merely a "tease" for the curious? How can such laws be enforced effectively?

5. What about a simple guideline which asks, "What would Jesus do?" Is it adequate? Is it useful?

6. As God in Christ provides forgiveness for all who fail to honor Him in their use of media or who fail to supervise the use of media by those for whom they are responsible, He provides us with the power of the Holy Spirit to make responsible choices with regard to media use. Apply each of the following passages to media use.

a. "Everything is permissible for me"—but not everything is beneficial. "Everything is permissible for me"—but I will not be mastered by anything. "Food for the stomach and the stomach for food"—but God will destroy them both. The body is not meant for immorality, but for the Lord, and the Lord for the body (1 Corinthians 6:12–13).

b. You, my brothers, were called to be free. But do not use your freedom to indulge the sinful nature; rather, serve one another in love (Galatians 5:13).

7. Explain the following statement in light of the responsibility of a parent to supervise their children's use of media: *Although your children may "outplay" you at video games, they still count on you to "know the score".*

Suggestions for Parents

Consider and discuss the following suggestions for forming constructive guidelines for the discriminating use of some media forms. It is important to recognize that at times, media usage can almost become almost addictive.

1. Encourage your child to *limit* time at any activity. After prolonged involvement in almost any form of media, but especially video games, children can become frustrated and possibly grouchy. Share an interesting and statistically proven fact—shorter playing times at video games tends to make for higher scores!

2. Encourage children to become selective and discriminating consumers. You can do this by what you do and by what you say. As a parent, become familiar with the media they use. Read reviews, *rent* games

before you buy, or borrow from someone else. Ask, "What kind of choices did the creator of the game make and what choices does the game, movie, or other form of entertainment encourage the user to make?" For example, how are women and minorities portrayed? Why are certain characters winning and others losing?

3. Make your own "media" using a group/social activity. Encourage game playing and movie watching to become a group rather than an individual activity. This allows for the input of others, especially in decision-making situations. View television together and show that you support positive programming. Advertisers can't afford to sponsor broadcasts that don't draw audiences. When you write or call them, you let them know how you and your group feel about what they are spending their advertising budgets on. And while you are talking to the sponsors and broadcasting stations, tell them what you would *like* to see. Remember, one person or a few *can* make a difference.

4. Communicate your preferences about programming to your local and regional lawmakers. Most people *assume* that others will do it for them. Discuss: Do you favor the manufacturing of televisions and cable terminals with built in time/channel "lock-out" circuitry? Either way, what have you done to be heard so that others won't make the decision for you?

Closing Meditation

Pray thanking God for the many different types of media available to us today. Ask for His guidance in using them to His glory.

It Is Written ▼

Opening Meditation

In John 5:39–40 Jesus chides the religious leaders of the time for missing the most important element of the Holy Scriptures. He says, "You diligently study the Scriptures because you think that by them you possess eternal life. These are the Scriptures that testify about Me." As we read and study the Bible, God desires us to see Jesus in His Word and to receive the salvation available only through Him. Pray a brief spontaneous prayer thanking God for His Word, the Bible, and for His living Word, Jesus.

What Do You Know about God?

God, our Creator and Redeemer, has revealed Himself to us in a variety of ways. Write several words telling what we can learn from each of the following about God.

1. mountains, wind, waves, and storms

2. delicate flowers, insects, and intricate human body parts

3. the universe

4. modern medical, agricultural, and scientific technology

5. the Bible

God's Word

From His created world we can learn much about God. But from the Bible alone we know that He sent His only Son, Jesus Christ, into the world to be our Savior from sin, death, and everlasting separation.

The Bible is God's great gift to us. John 20:31 records the reason God's Word was written. "But these are written that you may believe that Jesus is the Christ, the Son of God, and that by believing you may have life in His name."

Suppose that as you drive along one day you come upon an automobile accident. As you investigate, you notice one person, pinned in the car, apparently dying. Frightened, the person begins to ask you questions about God. What would you tell this person? Would you quote the Bible, or would you, in your own words, assure this person that Jesus loves them, and that believing, he or she will live with Christ forever?

Life with the Stranger

Read the following account of the stranger who came to live with a family and became a powerful influence in the home.

The Stranger

Before I was born, my father met a stranger whom he liked so much that he invited him to come live with our family. This stranger took to our home immediately and soon was just like one of the family. It seems like he was always present, and most members of the family were enchanted with him. Although Mom and Dad taught me to know and love God, this stranger also did some pretty important teaching. He was a storyteller and could weave the most fascinating tales. He could hold our entire family spellbound for hours on end. He seemed to know everything—about the world, and about us. The stories he told were so lifelike that he could make me laugh or cry.

He became much more than a stranger. He took my dad and I to our first major league baseball game. He took us to the movies and always made sure that we had a front row seat. This stranger/friend was an incessant talker. Dad didn't seem to mind, but mom would often get up and busy herself doing other things, even while our friend was talking.

In spite of the high moral values our family lived by, my parents didn't seem to mind when this new friend used an occasional unacceptable four-letter word. Although my dad squirmed and my mother looked away, I don't remember anyone ever confronting this new friend and telling him that his behavior was unacceptable. But I guess our friend figured that we needed to be exposed to different things. I began to wonder, because as time wore on, he even made cigars and cigarettes seem appealing. His talk about premarital and extramarital sex were blatant, suggestive, and to my mind, out of line. But in spite of my upbringing, I know that my early ideas about the way a man and woman ought to relate to one another was largely influenced by the ideas that this new friend brought into our home.

Looking back in perspective, I believe it was only by the grace of God that this stranger-become-friend did not influence me more. His ideals opposed the values of my friends and family, yet he never seemed to be confronted or was asked to leave our home.

More than 30 years have passed since this stranger moved into our home and became our friend. To me, he is not nearly so intriguing as he once was. But if you walked into my parents home, you would still find him sitting over in the corner, waiting for someone to listen.

Oh, his name? Well, we always just called him T V!

▼▼▼▼▼▼▼▼▼▼▼▼▼▼▼▼▼▼▼▼▼▼▼▼▼

1. List several ways that television is like a person invited to live with a family in their home.

2. List several ways television is unlike a person invited to live with a family in their home.

3. In the early 1950s a family gathered excitedly around the television set the father had just purchased and carried into the home. But the little girl in the family slipped away and went into her bedroom to cry. "Things will never be the same again," she sobbed. React to this incident.

Confronting Harmful Influences

Television and the technology that created it are gifts from our loving God to us. Much admirable and spiritually helpful information has been communicated through this powerful medium. Many have come to a saving faith in Jesus through the message of the Gospel transmitted in television waves. But television can also be a powerful tool of the devil. The forces of darkness would like nothing more than to succeed in using television and any other available means to encourage Christians to abandon their saving faith in Jesus.

Like us, Jesus was tempted to turn His back on His loving Father. While out in the desert one day, the devil urged Jesus to obey him and simply use His power to turn stones into bread (Matthew 4:3). Jesus' very first words of retort were, "It is written." Referring to the importance of sustenance, He said people "[do] not live on bread alone, but on every word that comes from the mouth of God!"

Comment on the following passages from Scripture, applying them to the spiritual nutrition God's people need as they face tempting, desensitizing influences in the world in which they live.

1. All Scripture is God-breathed and is useful for teaching, rebuking, correcting and training in righteousness, so that the man of God may be thoroughly equipped for every good work (2 Timothy 3:16–17).

2. All the prophets testify [including in their writings] that everyone who believes in Him receives forgiveness of sins through His name (Acts 10:43).

3. From infancy you have known the holy Scriptures, which are able to make you wise for salvation through faith in Christ Jesus (2 Timothy 3:15).

4. The Word of God . . . is at work in you who believe (1 Thessalonians 2:13).

5. Faith comes from hearing the message, and the message is heard through the word of Christ (Romans 10:17).

6. There is a way that seems right to a man, but in the end it leads to death (Proverbs 14:12).

Reading, Studying, and Living God's Word

The words "private devotions" mean a great deal to some people, and not very much to others. To have private devotions, means to devote a special time to God each day.

Proverbs 22:6 speaks of the importance of instruction in God's Word from an early age, including the promise, "Train a child in the way he should go, and when he is old he will not turn from it."

God does great things as His Spirit works through the Word, bringing people to saving faith and guiding, encouraging, and empowering them for the daily exercise of that faith. "So is My word that goes out from My mouth," says Isaiah 55:11, "It will not return to Me empty, but will accomplish what I desire and achieve the purpose for which I sent it."

Through the study and meditation on God's Word, His Holy Spirit strengthens our faith in Jesus. With a stronger faith comes the desire to live our faith in the things we think, say, and do. Write a phrase or two to comment on the positive and/or negative influences of television and other media forms on each of the following:

1. wise use of discretionary time

2. vocabulary development

3. exercise of problem-solving skills

4. awareness of the world around us

5. ability to relate to others

6. encouragement and motivation

Activities

1. Bring samples of devotional materials for the group to examine and consider for their personal use.

2. You don't have to wait until January 1 to make a resolution. Resolve to read through the entire Bible in one year. Review pages 14–16 for help.

3. Write a personal devotion of your own. Duplicate and distribute to the others in your study group.

4. Read Genesis 3:15. Before sin came into the world Adam and Eve talked *to* God. When Satan entered the picture, he began to talk *about* God. Discuss the difficulties that occur when people stop talking to God, and begin to talk about Him. Although it is not wrong to talk about God—which is the focus of much Bible study—we also need to talk to Him to maintain a close relationship with Him. If you are not already doing so, begin daily devotions with your family this week.

5. Read Romans 2:15. Because the requirements of God's law are written on our hearts doesn't mean that we no longer need the Bible. Only in the Bible has God revealed the coming of His Son, our Savior, Jesus.

Closing Meditation

Jesus said, "I am the way and the truth and the life. No one comes to the Father except through Me" (John 14:6). Close in prayer, asking God to help you to honor Him in your private and family devotions.

Evaluating Media **6** ▼

Opening Meditation

Ephesians 2:8–9 says, "For it is by grace you have been saved, through faith—and this is not from yourselves, it is the gift of God—not by works, so that no one can boast." Think for a moment about what it means to be saved. God tells us in His Word that we have been saved by grace rather than works (any goodness or good deeds on our part). Grace is God's undeserved love. To be saved by grace means that Christ has rescued us from being separated eternally from God.

We are also saved *for* something. Read each of the following passages and think for a moment about what God's saving action for you means for your life.

• But you are a chosen people, a royal priesthood, a holy nation, a people belonging to God, that you may declare the praises of Him who called you out of darkness into His wonderful light (1 Peter 2:9).

• The fruit of the Spirit is love, joy, peace, patience, kindness, goodness, faithfulness, gentleness and self-control (Galatians 5:22–23).

• Serve one another in love (Galatians 5:13).

• Direct me in the path of Your commands, for there I find delight. Turn my heart toward Your statutes and not toward selfish gain (Psalm 119:35–36).

• So whether you eat or drink or whatever you do, do it all for the glory of God (1 Corinthians 10:31).

Media and the Good Life

God has blessed each of us with a ready access to a vast variety of media. Books, magazines, newspapers, video, and television are popular and inexpensive. From the comfort of their homes, using a telephone or computer terminal, people can shop, swap, buy, sell, preview, and reject. Within seconds people can receive news of tragedies of epidemic proportions which once took months to surface. Before the election polling places are closed on the west coast of the U. S., news commentators on the east coast may have already predicted the winner of a political race.

Media informs, entertains, and motivates us, sometimes without our knowledge or consent. A number of years ago a certain movie theater tried an experiment. The individual frames of a motion picture pass by so rapidly that our eyes do not recognize individual frames. We see "motion" which is really a succession of still pictures "suggesting" motion. The theater spliced images of tempting beverages and snack treats into their regular feature movie. Without knowing why, that particular night moviegoers purchased many times more snacks than usual. The phenomena is called subliminal advertising. You can imagine why it was outlawed. But a point was well made. We are unconsciously affected by images and suggestions of which our subconscious mind is not even aware.

In recent years music, another powerful media, has been the unfortunate but violent battleground between parents and their children. Parents insist their children play their music much too loud and that the words are vile. Children insist they play the music and play it loudly because they enjoy the beat and that they don't even hear the words. Names of groups and the lifestyles they espouse and portray in music and on the covers of the tapes and CDs they have recorded offend and concern many parents.

Perhaps the most unfortunate part of this battleground between teens and parents is that it is often an undeclared war and an unfair fight. Both parents and teens need to enter a discussion about media with adequate information and a willingness to listen. Difficult and uncomfortable as it may be, parents can best serve their purpose by actually listening to the music or watching the movie *with* their teen. Only then can an intelligent discussion begin.

1. Apply each of the following passages to media as you endeavor to manage it for yourself and your family according to the new life that is yours by faith in Christ Jesus.

a. Do not be misled: "Bad company corrupts good character" (1 Corinthians 15:33).

b. But each one is tempted when, by his own evil desire, he is dragged away and enticed. Then, after desire has conceived, it gives birth to sin; and sin, when it is full-grown, gives birth to death (James 1:14–15).

c. Do not be overcome by evil, but overcome evil with good (Romans 12:21).

d. Godliness has value for all things, holding promise for both the present life and the life to come (1 Timothy 4:8).

e. For the grace of God that brings salvation has appeared to all men. It teaches us to say "No" to ungodliness and worldly passions, and to live self-controlled, upright and godly lives in this present age, while we wait for the blessed hope—the glorious appearing of our great God and Savior, Jesus Christ, who gave Himself for us to redeem us from all wickedness and to purify for Himself a people that are His very own, eager to do what is good (Titus 2:11–14).

2. A grandmother who had not been to a movie in quite some time, shared her shock over the language contained in a popular movie. The granddaughter who had treated her to the movie responded, "That's just the way it is Grandma! After all, it is rated 'R'!" Imagine you are in the room when this conversation is taking place. It is your turn to speak. What do you say?

Helpful Guidelines

In Philippians 4:8–9 Paul writes, "Finally, brothers, whatever is true, whatever is noble, whatever is right, whatever is pure, whatever is lovely, whatever is admirable—if anything is excellent or praiseworthy—think about such things." These words provide an excellent place for us to begin when evaluating media and its place in our life and in the lives of those with whom we live, work, and play.

But how can we determine or who decides what is excellent? How do we put out of our minds the terrible tragedy and injustice that fills our daily news in order to think about only those things that are right?

Fortunately, God has provided further direction for us in His holy Word. The Ten Commandments, for example, offer specific guidelines for our lives. Applying these commands of God to our lives, and putting them into practice as the power of the Holy Spirit enables us, guides us in choosing what is always in our best interest and in the best interest of others, as well.

1. Consider each of the Ten Commandments printed as follows. Restate each in your own words making a statement of commitment that includes no

negative words such as "no" or "not."(E.g., A commitment statement corresponding with the First Commandment would read, I will put God first in my life. Then jot a phrase or two telling how this commitment will affect your use of media.

The First Commandment
You shall have no other gods.

The Second Commandment
You shall not misuse the name of the Lord your God.

The Third Commandment
Remember the Sabbath day by keeping it holy.

The Fourth Commandment
Honor your father and your mother.

The Fifth Commandment
You shall not murder.

The Sixth Commandment
You shall not commit adultery.

The Seventh Commandment
You shall not steal.

The Eighth Commandment
You shall not give false testimony against your neighbor.

The Ninth Commandment
You shall not covet your neighbor's house.

The Tenth Commandment
You shall not covet your neighbor's wife, or his manservant or maidservant, his ox or donkey, or anything that belongs to your neighbor.

2. Some find it helpful when evaluating media to analyze the purpose behind the media presentation—are those responsible for what is read, seen, or heard endeavoring to inform, entertain, inspire or are they using media in order to shape opinions or sell? When is media appropriately used to shape opinions or sell? When is using media to shape opinions or to sell inappropriate?

3. In *Parenting Moral Teens in Immoral Times* (CPH, 1989), author and teacher Annette Frank makes the following suggestions for parents and teens as they deal with the issue of music media.

a. Begin with prayer for guidance and direction.

b. Recognize that popular music has changed significantly since most parents were the same age as their teens are now.

c. Music exercises a strong and invisible influence upon us. Music is carefully chosen for its effect upon people. The fads and styles that spin off from music groups and movies indicate that they do have a strong influence.

d. The clothing, actions, and words of many artists and actors convey strong messages which are often inconsistent with Christian values. Consider listening or watching with your teen and use this activity as a springboard for discussion about Christian values and their witness to Christ. Discuss the value of a popular saying—"Garbage in—garbage out!"

e. Help your teen find acceptable music and movies. Help them work with you to bring positive change in what is presented.

3. What additional benefits could result from helping your child make his or her choices in the use of media?

A Gift from God

Every good and perfect gift is from above, coming down from the Father of the heavenly lights, who does not change like shifting shadows. He chose to give us birth through the word of truth, that we might be a kind of firstfruits of all He created (James 1:17–18).

As surely as God gives good gifts, He will help us to use all with which we have been provided to His glory and for the benefit of ourselves and others. Rather than complain about the evils of media today, we can expend our energies in praising God for His many gifts. We can *use* media to His glory wherever possible. We can encourage the use of positive media for purposes for which we believe God intended it. Consider the list of types of media that follow. Write one or two examples of how each is or can be used to the glory of God and for the benefit of ourselves and others.

1. books

2. television and movies

3. radio

4. magazines and newspapers

5. computers

Closing Meditation

▲▲▲▲▲▲▲▲▲▲▲▲▲▲▲▲▲▲▲▲▲▲▲▲▲▲▲▲▲▲

May we Your precepts, Lord, fulfill
And do on earth our Father's will
As angels do above;
Still walk in Christ, the living way,
With all your children and obey
The law of Christian love.

So may we join Your name to bless,
Your grace adore, Your pow'r confess,
To flee from sin and strife.
One is our calling, one our name,
The end of all our hopes the same,
A glorious crown of life.

▼▼▼▼▼▼▼▼▼▼▼▼▼▼▼▼▼▼▼▼▼▼▼▼▼▼▼▼▼▼
▼

Session 1—Media, Messages, and My Family

▲ Focus

Welcome everyone. Give each participant a copy of the Study Guide. Encourage new participants to write their names on the front covers. Ask that they take the booklets home between sessions and bring them back each time the group meets.

▲ Objectives

That by the power of the Holy Spirit working through God's Word, the participants will

1. recognize and appreciate different kinds of media;
2. explore and appreciate more fully the various types of family units;
3. appreciate the importance and impact of media in the Christian family;
4. boldly confess God as their Creator and Caregiver, Jesus as their only Savior and Redeemer, and the Holy Spirit as the One who creates and sustains faith within them.

▲ Opening Devotion

Introduce the devotion saying, **God's Word is media; it communicates God's love for all people, telling of Jesus Christ, God's Word made flesh, who lived, died, and rose again to pay the penalty our sins deserved. By the power of His Holy Spirit working in us, we believe that God loves each of us, forgives our sins for Jesus' sake, and offers us eternal life.** Continue with the reading of Ps. 119:105, discussion, and the prayer.

▼

▲ What Is Media?

Underscore media as a means of communication. Continue with a discussion of the questions in this section as a large group.

1. Media is that which lies between two individuals or groups as they exchange ideas. Media communicates; it also entertains and inspires.

2. Invite participants to share types of media as you write them on the board or on a sheet of newsprint.

3. Invite participants to share their thoughts and ideas. List their responses in abbreviated form beside the list for item 2.

▲ The Changing Family

Read the first paragraph in this section aloud to the group. Invite participants to suggest various types of families in existence today. Possibilities include traditional, single-parent, blended, single adult, grandparents raising children, gay and lesbian couples with children, etc. Invite a volunteer to read the remaining paragraphs in this section. Ask participants to work in small groups of four to answer the questions in this section. After five minutes reassemble the whole group and review responses. Possibilities include the following.

1. Point out that by including a variety of family types in the stories they portray, television programs and movies help us to accept a variety of family types.

2. Society's acceptance of family types other than the traditional family helps members of such families to find support and greater understanding about the challenges and needs of persons in their situation. On the negative side, society's acceptance of alternative family configurations has positioned the traditional family as but one of several family options.

3. Answers may vary. Invite participants to offer opinions as to how well the church reaches out to those who are living in families with a configuration that differs from the traditional family consisting of two parents and one or more children.

4. God's Word tells us to take a firm stand against lifestyles that go against His will for us (e.g., You shall not commit adultery forbids persons who are not married to each other to form households.) However, we take a stand against

sin so that as the Holy Spirit works through God's Word, sinners may come to repentance and therefore be ready to receive the comfort of the assurance that in Christ their sins are all forgiven.

▲ Media and Our Way of Life

After introducing this section with the two brief paragraphs at the beginning, ask participants to work in pairs or in groups of three or four to respond to the numbered items. After seven to ten minutes, reassemble the group and briefly invite comments about one or more of the items.

1. On a piece of paper, invite each group member to list the different media which they have used or viewed during the past 24 hours. Possibilities include the following: television, movies, newspaper, radio, books, magazines, videos, electronic bulletin boards, tapes, CDs, etc. Compare lists and talk about availability or accessibility. For example, some may have cable TV and others not. Some may receive one daily paper and others two. Some may have a personal computer in their home and others not. Ask, **Are some families media deficient? Do you believe there are "minimum" kinds of media which families/children should have access to?**

2. Answers will vary. If you choose, sample the group to see which form of media they value the most.

3–5. Answers will vary. Engage the group in a discussion about what they perceive to be the greatest problem which faces families today concerning the use of media? Talk about obsession with or overuse of one kind of media, such as video games or televisions. Ask, **Is this just a problem with young people?** Obviously many adults become couch potatoes when it comes to some media, such as entertainment television, movies, or games. Discuss ideas that participants have tried to limit or redirect media use of both children and adults.

▲ Media and You

1–2. Invite group members to share what they would save in the event of a fire. Ask which of the items they would save are media. Possible responses include family pictures, scrapbooks, and books.

59

3. Affirm the value of the articles because they communicate the love family members have one for the other.

4. Point out that God's Word is the most important and valuable of all media. The way in which it was written singles it out from all other writing; God inspired certain people, and used their ordinary words, so that we could know and communicate important spiritual truths. The truth of God's Word depends upon His authorship. The value of God's Word rests in its saving message—Jesus Christ is the Son of God and Savior of the world.

Examples of the neglect of God's Word include failure to read, study, and meditate upon God's Word in personal lives, failure to attend corporate worship, and by showing disrespect for God and His Word.

5. Affirm God's forgiveness in Christ for all sins—including those of the misuse of God's Word and of other forms of media.

6. As the Spirit of God works through the Gospel in the lives of those who love and trust in Him, God brings them to communicate His Word because it is a) the means to faith and a new life in Christ and b) useful in the Christian life for teaching, rebuking, correcting, and training in righteousness.

7. Encourage participants to share their ideas.

8–9. Although the Gospel is God's message, He has entrusted to us the sharing of that message. He has also given us differing gifts which we may use, creatively, so that many more may know the saving love of God in Christ.

During the discussion of these questions, highlight the importance of sharing faith in Christ and ways to eliminate some of the things which impede the spread of the Gospel. As leader, share some of the ways in which you share your faith with others and encourage others to do so both now, during your sessions, and later in their daily Christian lives.

▲ Share a Word

Allow several minutes for participants to respond individually to these items. Invite volunteers to share their responses with the whole group. Affirm God's Word as His living message of hope, the means through which the Holy Spirit empowers God's people with strength and direction for daily living.

Encourage use of God's Word through regular Bible reading. Your group might agree to try the suggested daily Bible reading schedule for the duration of the study, and share their feelings as you go along.

▲ Closing Meditation

Conclude the session following the suggestion in the Study Guide.

Session 2—The Great Escape

▲ Focus

Welcome everyone. Make sure each participant has a copy of the Study Guide. Encourage participants to write their names on the front covers. Ask that they take the booklets home between sessions and bring them back each time the group meets.

▲ Objectives

That by the power of the Holy Spirit working through God's Word, the participants will

1. give thanks to God for the many different forms of media with which He has blessed them;

2. acknowledge the variety and difference in media forms, as God has given them, and affirm many possible alternatives available to them;

3. study and discuss ways to encourage others to use these alternatives;

4. affirm the importance of media for informing, entertaining, and inspiring God's people.

▲ Opening Meditation

Begin with the Bible reading and prayer as suggested in the Study Guide.

▲ Media

If you choose to do so, acquire a copy of Chris Van Allsburg's *The Wretched Stone*, available from most public libraries. Begin by reading and discussing the book. The crew, obsessed with "the wretched stone" changed into monkeys and abandoned their tasks, which led inevitably to a shipwreck. Ask, **What is the author of this children's book saying to you? Was he effective? How would you use this to help others begin to think about the effects of TV?**

Ask participants to complete the activity in this section individually. Invite comments about the use of media in their homes. Comment on both positive and negative aspects of media. Affirm media and the information, entertainment, and ability to communicate provided through media as gifts from our loving God. Continue with the next section.

▲ Two Perspectives

Tell participants to keep the positive and negative aspects of media in mind as they work through this section. Read the introductory paragraphs to the class. Then ask them to work with partners or in groups of three or four to apply each of the references to the influence of media in their lives. When groups have finished, reassemble the large group and review responses.

1. The group may cite positive examples of media where sacrificial actions of love by one person for another are presented or described in a dramatic way. Coarse joking and other talk or actions that demean God's gift of sexuality, or disregard God's design for reserving sexual intercourse for marriage are perhaps more prevalent.

2. Affirm examples of media used to the glory of God, such as watching a television program about the natural world might help a Christian viewer appreciate the intricate planning and careful design evidenced by the Creator in the world He made for us. Negative applications include media that contains pornography and/or promotes or glorifies satanic or demonic arts, greed, or selfishness.

3. Hearts set on things above—on serving and honoring Him who died for us and rose again—are those that by the Spirit's power work to bring the good news of the Gospel to

those who do not yet believe. Encourage the group to share examples of how the Gospel is able to reach individuals and nations through the use of various media—radio, television, printed matter. Negative examples should focus on any use of media to glorify or promote the sinful things of this world.

4. Positive examples would center on the use of media to do the will of God, such as using video or printed materials to study God's Word or reflect upon His goodness to us. Negative examples would include any use of media to tempt people to be self-absorbed or focused on the good life at the expense of the goals and work of the kingdom of God.

5. Positive examples will emphasize qualities either compatible with or evidencing the standards of behavior God has established for those who love and trust in Him. Negative examples include the focus of media on the dark side of human nature. Some media presentations may experiment with topics and formats that are counterproductive to the welfare of both individuals and society for the sole purpose that these things have never been presented before (e.g., material that contains graphic violence, satanic arts, sexually explicit scenes).

Conclude this section, stressing that the good news of Jesus Christ offers both forgiveness for past failures and direction for future media use.

▲ Wise Use of Media

Ask one or more volunteers to take turns reading the material in this section aloud to the group, paragraph by paragraph. Talk about ways in which television is a great escape. People can escape into it, and parents can escape parenting responsibilities by simply allowing their children to be entertained by it. There is a difference between escaping "from" and escaping "to." Invite individuals to express their feelings about how television (and other media) can simply become a background.

Ask, **When you don't like what is on the menu (TV program listings), do you still tend to watch (and listen and think) especially if someone else enjoys what is being presented?** Talk about the almost hypnotic nature of television, and how peer pressure often influences our decisions about *whether* to watch, and *what* to watch! Television is like a "plug in drug" which can rob massive amounts of time. Invite those who might have grown up without television to share what families did with their Saturday mornings, for example, before TV. What did young couples do on dates before movies?

Invite their comments about a mother who allowed her five-year-old to watch "Beavis and Butthead" on MTV. From this program, he got the idea that "fire is cool." Invite group comments about a recently enacted "Children's Television Act" requiring television stations, when renewing their licenses, to demonstrate that advertising aired on their stations serve "the educational needs" of their young viewers. Ask, **Do you believe this will solve some problems? Whose responsibility is it to monitor the viewing habits of children?**

Proceed with a discussion of the questions in this section.

1–2. Invite participant comments about the concern over the amount of violence on television. Brainstorm responsible Christian action to promote healthy, wholesome use of media.

Consider what is being done in your local area to teach children to become "discriminating consumers" of media who are equipped to ask and answer questions such as, "Is this worth my time?"

3. Help the group to begin thinking about possible alternatives. Creativity necessary to think about such possibilities can be stifled by the strong suggestions of television, especially when it is almost omnipresent. Expand this through some of the recommended activities, both as a group, and later at home. Perhaps you could begin the next session by talking about the results of alternative-suggesting.

Comment on Dr. Koop's quote. The "dark side" is an accurate picture of sinful nature, and while we don't have to look at it all the time, it does sell advertising and movie tickets. Consider ways to be heard by those who determine programming.

▲ During the Week

Encourage participants to do one or more of these activities during the coming week.

▲ Closing Meditation

Follow the directions provided in the Study Guide.

Session 3—Think about Such Things!

▲ Focus

Welcome everyone. Make sure each participant has a copy of the Study Guide. Encourage participants to write their names on the front covers. Ask that they take the booklets home between sessions and bring them back each time the group meets.

▲ Objectives

That by the power of the Holy Spirit working through God's Word, the participants will

1. express confident trust that God sustains and guides their everyday lives, and that the forgiving love of Christ is always available to them;

2. identify sources of violence in our world;

3. recognize the danger violence presents to individuals;

4. respond to violence in media in ways that give glory to God.

▲ A Threat to Society

Use the questions to initiate a discussion of the quote by Payton. Mention that those who "lock up" their televisions must be willing to be without the positive aspects of television, such as news, family entertainment, and helpful information.

▲ Sex and Violence in Media

Invite one or more volunteers to read the material in this section aloud to the group, pausing between paragraphs to add pertinent comments. Continue with a discussion of the questions in this section.

1. Point out that issues of censorship are complex.

2. God's people set standards based on God's Word, not according to what is deemed acceptable by media or the society in which we live. We can avoid becoming desensitized by making regular and continuous use of God's Word and the Sacraments.

3. Christian families can stress and promote activities in the home and outside the home that involve people actively in interaction and personal growth, such as games, athletics, service projects, and hobbies.

4. Allow participants to share about the control they exercise over their children's use of media. Participants are likely to identify peer influences and the pressures of society as forces working against their attempts to control the influences that touch the lives of their children.

▲ How Do You Picture Jesus?

Read Mark 10:13–16 to the group. Then proceed with the questions in this section.

1–2. Invite participants to share images of Jesus they would include if they were making a movie about Jesus. Most people prefer to think of God and His great love for us and for all people.

3. The Bible does *describe* violent acts. But even in His removal of evil influences from the world God is working to save for Himself those who love and trust in Him.

4. God has two sides—His justice and His mercy. The Law and Gospel, as revealed in Scriptures, reflect the two sides of God's love. And His hard side, the Law is not evil. It merely reflects His holy and just will. Because God is just, He must punish sin. God continues to offer His mercy to sinners through faith in Christ Jesus' atoning sacrifice for sin—His death on the cross.

5. The Bible speaks plainly and directly about evil and its effects on the good world God created. Nowhere does God condone evil. Neither does He encourage us to hurt or harm ourselves, others, or the world He has made for us. Often God describes what others have done in order to warn us of the consequences of sinful behavior.

▲ God's Gifts

Read the introductory paragraphs in this section to the group. Stress that violence and the misuse of God's gift of sexuality are not God's doing. Rather they are results of the fall into sin. Continue with the activity. Invite participants to share with partners or in small groups the gifts God gives to heal and restore fallen humanity. Recap the discussion in the large group.

1. a. One day when God brings an end to the world and its existence as we know it, He will restore for those who know and believe in Him the perfect peace that existed in Eden as this passage from Isaiah describes it.

b. Until God comes to remove us from this sinful world, He blesses those who believe in Him with a peace that those still held in the grasp of sin cannot fathom. This peace gives Christians strength, courage, and perseverance.

2. The additional gift from God, described in Romans 8:18–25 is hope—a hope that enables believers, even now, to see and anticipate the heavenly home that awaits them.

▲ God's Presence in the Lives of His People

Introduce this section, pointing out that by faith the Holy Spirit changes us so that we no longer desire to emulate or follow the ways of the world. Invite participants to work through this section with partners or in their small groups before reviewing responses as a whole group.

1. Since we have been raised with Christ, God's people can set their hearts on things above, where Christ is seated at the right hand of God. Because our natural self has died, our new self is now hidden with Christ in God. We can now live knowing that when Christ, who is our life, appears, we also will appear with Him in glory.

2. Evidences of the old self include: sexual immorality, impurity, lust, evil desires, and greed which is idolatry, anger, rage, malice, slander, and filthy language. Evidences of the new self include: compassion; kindness; humility; gentleness; patience; bearing with one another; forgiving one another as God has forgiven us, love; letting the peace of Christ dwell in us; being thankful; letting the Word of Christ

dwell in us as we teach and admonish one another with all wisdom and as we sing psalms, hymns, and spiritual songs with gratitude in our hearts to God; and doing everything in the name of the Lord Jesus giving thanks to the Father through Him.

3 a–b. Accept participants' responses.

c. Affirm and encourage responses that focus on using media in ways that give glory and honor to the name of the Lord and encourage and promote an attitude of gratitude toward Him for all He has done for and given to us.

4. As the Spirit of God works in the lives of His people through the means of grace—the Word and the Sacrament—we already see ourselves living in heaven. He desires and motivates us to live focused on the reward that is already ours by faith in Christ Jesus.

▲ During the Week

Encourage participants to do one or more of these activities during the week ahead.

▲ Closing Meditation

Conclude your lesson following the directions included in this section of the Study Guide.

Session 4—What about Censorship?

▲ Focus

Welcome everyone. Make sure each participant has a copy of the Study Guide. Encourage participants to write their names on the front covers. Ask that they take the booklets home between sessions and bring them back each time the group meets.

▲ Objectives

That by the power of the Holy Spirit working through God's Word, the participants will

1. demonstrate a desire to rely more fully upon the activity of God in Christ in their daily lives;

2. acknowledge the sensitive and complex issues which accompany censorship and the restraint and repression of any form of media;

3. recognize that while every individual practices some form of censorship, persons in authoritative positions must exercise greater care and discrimination in making blanket decisions;

4. respond cautiously to any overtures of censorship, bearing in mind the spirit of the Fifth Commandment.

▲ Opening Meditation

Follow the directions provided in the Study Guide.

▲ Think on Those Things!

Invite a participant to read the paragraphs in this section or read them aloud to the group yourself. Invite participants to reflect upon what they have heard and read, contributing examples or comments on the evil each of us has within and also on Christ's forgiving, healing, and ennobling power at work within those who belong to Him.

▲ Controlling What Is Seen and Heard

Review with participants these excerpts from history regarding censorship. Reflect on the struggles various societies have had with this difficult problem. Comment that all of us practice censorship in some form. Continue with a discussion of the questions provided in this section.

1. Answers may vary. Participants are likely to agree that no single individual should have the sole authority to censor material for a society, as was the case in ancient Rome. Point out that at times banning objectionable media presentations seems to promote rather than discourage interest in them.

2–4. Again, answers will vary. Encourage whole group sharing.

5. Invite participants to read the Bible references printed in the Study Guide silently and to reflect upon one or more of them.

Stimulate discussion by referring to Romans 12:9, "Hate what is evil; cling to what is good." Say, **Who determines what is good and evil? Is it sufficient to say God's Word is our guide or are guidelines for specific application necessary?**

▲ Responsibility and the Right of Choice

Read or invite a member of the group to read the material in this section. Comment that supervising the media to which children are exposed falls under the realm of parental responsibility, but caution against dealing with censorship in a simplistic way. Recall times when the Bible and other Christian literature was banned and burned.

Stress God's sovereign control over all that takes place within His creation. Comment that Voltaire, a noted 18th-century French philosopher, bragged that although it had taken 17 centuries to build Christianity, within a generation or two it would become extinct and forgotten. Ironically, 20 years after his death, his printing press was sold to the Geneva Bible Society for the production of Bibles and other Christian material. Consider similar claims by the popular rock music group the Beatles, who at one point bragged that they were more important than Jesus. And where are they now?

Continue with the questions. Invite participants to review the questions in groups of three or four. With the whole group invite comments or insights that surfaced during the small group sharing.

1. Answers will vary. Comment that in His Word God encourages those who belong to Him to encourage one another in those activities and influences in accordance with God's will so that together we may grow in grace and bring glory and honor to His name. In the case of Christian parents, teaching children to evaluate and discriminate among those influences they allow into their lives is a much greater and

70
▼

much more challenging task than simply prohibiting certain materials.

2. Accept participants responses.

3. Responses should focus on the intent of the magazine in showing pictures of fully or partially naked people.

4. Allow participants to express their opinions. Ask the group to consider the question, "When is it appropriate for parents to view a movie in advance of deciding whether to allow their children to view it?"

5. Comment that many have found it helpful, when considering an activity, to ask themselves whether they would invite Jesus to take part in that activity with them.

6. a–b. Applications of these passages should focus on the freedom we have in Christ to choose only those things that will be of eternal value and benefit.

7. Comments should relate to the God-given obligation of parents to assert themselves in guiding their children in their use of media as well as in all other areas. Those in authority must give an account to God (Heb. 13:17; 1 Peter 4:5).

▲ Suggestions for Parents

Introduce this section by discussing how we best teach young people to make responsible decisions regarding media use. Point out that we teach a great deal by the way we live. All Christians can model God-pleasing behavior to others. Encourage group members to read the suggestions in this section. Invite participants to share their own suggestions of what they are doing or would like to try. Urge them to try one or more of the suggestions with their families. Encourage them to bring feedback to share at the next session.

Talk about addiction to certain kinds of media. Although we are most familiar with addiction to substances, such as alcohol or drugs, medical science also recognizes something called process addiction. When pleasure is derived from a process, it will be repeated so often that it can cause problems in relationships.

▲ Closing Meditation

Follow directions provided in the Study Guide.

▼

Session 5—It Is Written

▲ Focus

Welcome everyone. Make sure each participant has a copy of the Study Guide. Encourage participants to write their names on the front covers. Ask that they take the booklets home between sessions and bring them back each time the group meets.

▲ Objectives

That by the power of the Holy Spirit working through God's Word, the participants will

1. affirm God's power, working especially through the written Word of God, to make His people "wise for salvation through faith in Jesus Christ" (2 Timothy 3:15);

2. explore the power and impact of print media as an alternative form;

3. celebrate the variety of ways in which God conveys important messages to His people through media;

4. use media in their devotional life.

▲ What Do You Know about God?

Say, **Media informs, entertains, and inspires. In this session you will be talking more about the informational and inspirational aspects of media—specifically print media.** Begin by inviting participants to complete the opening activity with a partner or in small groups. Recap responses after reassembling the large group. Possible responses follow.

1. These reveal God's power, might, and majestic beauty.

2. These show God to be the ultimate designer who gives careful attention to even the most minute of details.

3. God is vast, without limits in all aspects of Himself, including intelligence, abilities, power, and love.

4. God gives people, the crown of His creation, many abilities and discoveries to enhance their lives and to use to His glory. These abilities and discoveries hint at the awesome knowledge and capabilities He possesses.

5. The Bible identifies the one true God as the Trinity. It tells us about God's love for all people and the saving work of Jesus to redeem fallen humanity and to free us from the punishment our sins deserved. The Bible provides specific information about the three persons of the Godhead and about the coming to earth of God's Son as a human being to live, die, and rise again to save us.

▲ God's Word

Read the material in this section to the group. Comment that God's Word has been written for our salvation and the salvation of all people. Invite participants to share what they would say to the dying person.

Comment that in such a situation a person could witness to the dying person by reciting or paraphrasing John 3:16, inserting the person's name in appropriate places in order to personalize it.

▲ Life with the Stranger

Invite one or more participants to read the paragraphs of "The Stranger." Proceed with a discussion of the questions that follow it.

1–3. Encourage whole group sharing. Welcome reminiscences about days before television. Accept participants' comments. Affirm the great change that media, such as television, has brought to us individually and as a society. Affirm comments about positive changes as well as comments about negative ones.

▲ Confronting Harmful Influences

Read or have a volunteer read the paragraphs in this section.

If time permits, read the entire account of Jesus' temptation in Matthew 4:1–11. Underscore the importance of making regular and continual use of God's Word for the faith-sustaining power and encouragement the Holy Spirit brings us through it.

Discuss Jesus' resistance of the devil's temptations with portions of God's Word. At the devil's first enticement Jesus responded, "Man does not live on bread alone, but on every word that comes from the mouth of God" (Matthew 4:4). Remind participants of the days when God's people traveled from Egypt to the Promised Land. As they wandered in the wilderness, God provided manna, but only one day at a time (Ex. 16). By providing manna one day at a time, God showed His people their constant dependence upon Him. He wanted them to know that they couldn't go it alone. Similarly, through the ongoing use of His Word, God sustains us spiritually for the challenges and rigors of each new day.

Talk about the Fifth Petition of the Lord's Prayer, "Give us today our daily bread" (Matt. 6:11). According to Luther, daily bread includes *everything* we need to support our body and life. Therefore when we pray this petition, we are also asking that God gives us the comfort, strength, and direction provided only through His Word.

Invite participants to work with partners or in small groups to apply each of the passages in this section to our need for the spiritual strength God brings us through His Word as we contend with the influences within us and in the world around us that work against the blessings of life and faith God desires to bring us. After several minutes reassemble the large group and invite comments.

1. God's Word equips us for every good work and enables those who use it to teach, rebuke, correct, and train others in the way that is right.

2. God's Word provides assurance that Jesus has forgiven all sins through His all-sufficient life, death, and resurrection for us.

3. God's Word tells of the salvation all may freely receive through faith in Christ Jesus.

4. God's Word originates faith-evidencing thoughts, words, and actions in the lives of those who believe.

5. The saving faith comes from the outside, as it is shared with others.

6. Refer to the story of "The Stranger." Comment that the norms of society cannot—nor will not ever be—God's desired norms for His people. Only God, working through His Word, can equip us to honor Him as we manage media and all other influences.

74

▲ Reading, Studying, and Living God's Word

Comment on the good things God brings into the lives of those who regularly read and study God's Word. Allow time for participants to complete the activity in this section individually. Then allow participants to comment to the group about one or more of these items. Affirm both positive and negative responses. Mention that most of us neglect reading God's Word and talking to Him in prayer when we use media solely for purposes of entertainment and to pass the time. Comment that at times using God's Word together with information and resources the media provides has distinct benefits, making us aware of current challenges and needs to which we may apply the principles and energies God has given us to use for Him.

▲ Activities

Introduce this section comparing the benefits of group Bible study with those of individual or family devotions. Small group Bible study helps us to grow in our faith together with other believers as we learn from God's Word and from one another. But in individual or family devotions, God speaks to us as individuals or families, listening to our personal thoughts and concerns and answering the questions of our heart.

Comment on how busy schedules can preclude devotions. Talk also about how Bible reading and devotions may be awkward to people because it is an unfamiliar task. Share your personal struggles.

Share materials you have found useful in your daily Bible reading and devotions, including *Portals of Prayer* for adults, *My Devotions* for families, and *Happy Times* for families with little children. Christian bookstores display literally hundreds of excellent devotional books in which other Christians have related their understanding of Holy Scripture to their daily walk. There are devotions for teens, for new moms, for the divorced, and unemployed. Many good devotionals are available for singles and widowed. Encourage group members to share the titles and other information about resources which they have found particularly helpful. You may wish to

▼

raid the shelves of your church or pastor's library for additional titles. It is always helpful to actually *show* people what a particular resource looks like.

Encourage participants to do one or more of the activities in this section.

▲ Closing Meditation

Following directions provided in the Study Guides.

Session 6—Evaluating Media

▲ Focus

Welcome everyone. Make sure each participant has a copy of the Study Guide.

▲ Objectives

That by the power of the Holy Spirit working through God's Word, the participants will

1. boldly and freely confess faith in Jesus Christ as the Lord of their lives and their Savior from sin, death, and everlasting separation from God;

2. acknowledge ways in which media may be used to the glory of God and for the benefit of themselves and others;

3. reflect the need to evaluate the usefulness and appropriateness of all media;

4. gain an appreciation for evaluating media for themselves and others around them.

▲ Opening Devotions

Demonstrate your joy over all that God in Christ has done for you as you lead the opening devotion. Read or paraphrase the opening paragraph. Then invite participants to comment on the purpose(s) for which God has saved them according to the Bible references provided in the Study Guides. Stress the new-life goals and objectives God's Spirit brings to those who believe.

Mention that in today's session we will explore how we can evaluate and use media for purposes that honor and glorify God.

▲ Media and the Good Life

Read or invite a participant to read the material in this section aloud. Pause or ask the reader to pause between paragraphs so that you may comment about what has just been read. Stress the blessing that God has brought to all people through the technological advancements that has made possible the variety and quality of media that is so much a part of our daily lives. Invite participants to comment on these blessings as well as on the negative effects of media. Proceed with numbered items for discussion. Invite participants to work either in pairs or in groups of three or four. Then reassemble everyone for a whole group review of the discussion.

1. Following are possible applications of the passages to the management of media by those who trust in Jesus as their Savior.

a. Bad company corrupts good character. Many use media as a form of company. Negative influences of media correlate highly to the negative influence a friend or acquaintance might have in a person's life.

b. Just as the Holy Spirit works within God's people to change us by the power of the saving Gospel, temptations work to gain an inner hold on us so that we, the people of God, may be led to turn our backs on God and give ourselves completely over to the powers of death. Tempting influences are far from harmless.

c. God desires His people to rely upon His power to overcome the evil influence of the world in which we live with the goodness He enables us both to have and to bring into lives of those around us.

d. The power God gives us to bring our thoughts, desires, and actions into line with His own has present as well and eternal benefits, because God only desires and demands what is best for us.

e. In His grace God teaches us to avoid and reject ungodly

77

and worldly influences and to live self-controlled, upright, and godly lives. Point out that God gives His people this knowledge, power, and understanding through His Word and Sacrament.

2. Accept participant responses, affirming comments that point to the need to protect ourselves as God's people from becoming desensitized to the evil in the world around us as we witness to the Lord who bought us from the power of evil at the cost of His very life. Ask the group to explain the following saying in light of this discussion, "If ten thousand people say a foolish thing, it is still a foolish thing." The grandmother's shock over the content of the movie is perhaps a more appropriate response than the casual acceptance of language and dramatizations of behaviors that offend against God and His will for us.

▲ Helpful Guidelines

Read or ask a volunteer to read the introductory paragraphs in this section. Underscore that the guidelines presented in Phil. 4:8–9 suggest that God's people think about those things that are true, noble, right, pure, lovely, admirable, excellent, or praiseworthy. Explain that the Ten Commandments provide the context for dwelling on these concepts. Continue with the activities. Stress that only as the Spirit of God motivates and enables us can we desire to adopt and follow through on any commitment to honor God with lives of obedience to Him. Invite participants to work independently to complete item one. Then discuss items 2 and 3 as a whole group.

1. Answers will vary. Consider the following as possibilities for the second and third columns.

The First Commandment—I will put God first in my life—I will choose and support media that glorifies God and either explains or applies the true teaching and application of His Word or is helpful in some other way to the spiritual life and development of myself and those whom I love.

The Second Commandment—I will honor God's name—I will use and choose media to assist in my life of worship, praise, and prayer and to proclaim the victory of God in Christ over the satanic powers.

The Third Commandment—I will honor God's Word—I will support the use of media for purposes of worship, study,

78

and mediation and to spread the Good News of salvation by grace through faith in Jesus.

The Fourth Commandment—I honor those God has placed into positions of authority over me—I will choose media that shows proper respect for parents, the elderly, government officials, pastors, and others in authority.

The Fifth Commandment—I will love and help others—I will endeavor to learn and understand from media about others and their needs so that I may better reach out to them with the love of Christ.

The Sixth Commandment—I will respect marriage and human sexuality—I will choose decent reading material, television programs, videos, and movies and encourage others to choose the same.

The Seventh Commandment—I will help others to protect and improve their income and possessions—I will choose media that shows proper respect for the rights of others.

The Eighth Commandment—I will defend and speak well of others and will explain everything in the kindest way—I will seek positive influences, endeavoring to learn from, rather than delight in, the mistakes of others.

The Ninth Commandment—I will be content with the possessions God has given me—I will seek contentment with God's gifts, using media to make the best use of the resources God has provided.

The Tenth Commandment—I will be content with the servants God has provided—I will use media to promote and encourage faithfulness in a response to God's faithfulness to us in Christ Jesus.

2. Answers will vary. Media has made possible the rapid spread of the Gospel and other news, information, and presentations of great benefit, interest, and enjoyment to people everywhere. On the other hand, much harm has been done through the years with the use of media in spreading harmful propaganda, pornography, and other exploitive material.

3. Invite parents to share their struggles and joys of parenting as they deal with issues of music media. Ask, **How does the forgiveness, acceptance, and love of Christ move us to change the way we approach music and other sensitive issues between parents and their children?**

Additional benefits resulting from parents and children

dealing together with music and other media-related issues may include growing together in an understanding of what are and are not helpful influences in the life of a Christian, a deepening parent/child relationship, and growth for both parent and child in decision making that honors God.

▲ A Gift from God

Read the introductory paragraph to the group. Stress the variety of wonderful ways in which God continues to shower His blessings upon His people. Allow several minutes for participants to work in pairs or in small groups to complete the activity in this section. Then reassemble the whole group for general sharing about how these types of media may be used in ways that honor God and benefit ourselves and others.

▲ Closing Meditation

Read or sing the stanzas of "May We Your Precepts, Lord, Fulfill" printed in the Study Guide. Encourage participants to think specifically about media and its use in their lives as they pray the words together.